GW01036149

IEA LECTUR

Unemployment versus Inflation?

An Evaluation of the Phillips Curve

MILTON FRIEDMAN

Paul Snowden Russell Distinguished Service
Professor of Economics, University of Chicago

With a British Commentary

'The End of "Demand Management":

How to Reduce Unemployment in the Late 1970s'

by

DAVID E. W. LAIDLER

Professor of Economics,
University of Manchester

Published by
THE INSTITUTE OF ECONOMIC AFFAIRS
1975

First published June 1975
by
THE INSTITUTE OF ECONOMIC AFFAIRS

SBN 255 36069 – X

Printed in Great Britain by
GIBBONS BARFORD, WOLVERHAMPTON
Set in Monotype Plantin

Contents

BRITISH COMMENTARY
The End of 'Demand Management':
How to Reduce Unemployment in the 1970s

Preface

THE INSTITUTE has inaugurated a series of lectures by economists, and also by economic historians and other social scientists, to discuss fundamental aspects of the British economy and developments in economic thinking that help to shed light on them.

IEA Lecture No. 1 was delivered in 1973 by Dr Charles Hanson of the University of Newcastle on the British labour market and its development through a century of trade union legislation culminating in the 1971 Industrial Relations Act. It was published as Occasional Paper 38.[1]

IEA Lecture No. 2 was delivered in 1974 (September) by Professor Milton Friedman of the University of Chicago on a different, but related, aspect of the labour market: the fundamental interconnections between unemployment and inflation. It took the form of an analysis of the developing debate among economists on what has become known as 'the Phillips Curve' devised in 1958 by the late Professor A. W. Phillips (1914-1975) to show the relationship between unemployment and the rate of change of wages over time. Work on preparation of the papers emerging from the IEA seminar on inflation, also in September 1974, to which Professor Friedman contributed notably,[2] delayed the processing of his lecture. He revised an imperfect transcript of the tape-recording in December and generously re-created the drawings of diagrams he had used in the lecture. He also corrected a series of answers to questions, which appear here as the Appendix on 'The Trade Unions and Inflation'.

Professor Friedman's revised lecture is published mainly for the interest of economists and students of economics. Although it is composed with his customary verbal skill and felicity, it is concerned with a theorem that will be unfamiliar to readers who have not followed the academic debate on the Phillips Curve but that is germane to the understanding of the relationship between inflation and unemployment. Since the lecture was originally delivered to an audience primarily of economists, Professor Friedman used mathe-

---

[1] *Trade Unions: A Century of Privilege?*

[2] IEA Readings No. 14, *Inflation: Causes, Consequences, Cures*, 1974.

matical notations and technical terms that are familiar to specialists but that will seem forbidding to non-economists. What is important for laymen is the implications of the debate for policy. Professor Friedman touches on them briefly in section VI. To emphasise the importance of the theoretical analysis and its relevance for recent, and possibly impending, developments in the British economy, we invited Professor David Laidler of the University of Manchester (soon unhappily, with his close colleague, Professor Michael Parkin, to be lost to Britain but gained by Canada in the international free market for economists) to re-interpret and present the discussion in non-technical prose for non-economists with the special interests and anxieties of British readers in mind.

It is therefore hoped that the *Paper* will be of value not only to the increasing number of specialists reached by IEA *Papers* but also to economists and students of economics who follow the continuing debate on the Phillips Curve and to non-economists in industry, government, public life and press and television who want to know what economists are debating that can shed light on the working, or non-working, of the economic system.

The most important conclusions of the argument are that inflation can remove (some) unemployment in the short run but not in the long run; that monetary policy is incapable of removing the unemployment caused by the real institutional or structural obstacles to the absorption of labour, measured by what economists, following Friedman, call the 'natural' rate of unemployment;[1] that the post-war attempts, following Keynesian teaching, to do so have produced inflation; that the theory of 'demand management' which has inspired post-war Conservative and Labour policy and dominated Treasury advice is invalid; and that attention must be increasingly directed to the institutional reform of the labour market.

The whole discussion is sobering since it points to reforms in long-standing British institutions, and not less in political, academic and trade union attitudes, that will be even more difficult to achieve

[1] The *locus classicus* of this term is Professor Friedman's Presidential Address to the American Economic Association in December 1967, 'The Role of Monetary Policy', printed in the *American Economic Review*, March 1968: 'The "natural rate of unemployment" . . . is the level that . . . [reflects] the structural characteristics of the labour and commodity markets, including market imperfections, stochastic variability in demands and supplies, the cost of gathering information about job vacancies and labour availabilities, the costs of mobility, and so on.'

than the accompanying changes in the institutions of money and monetary policy.

But it is also encouraging since it sheds clearer light on avoidable unemployment in Britain and on the ways of removing it. If resistance to labour market reform can end only in industrial confrontation and the collapse of the open society, the possibly happy way out of what seems a cruel dilemma may have to lie in a new attitude to, and new policies on, unemployment. The Keynesian era, begun in the early 1930s slump, taught a generation of students, economists, politicians, civil servants and journalists that the supreme evil was unemployment, and that economic thinking and political action should be directed above all to removing it. The lesson, as interpreted by the Keynesians, was that (a little) inflation could remove (a lot of) unemployment. But this teaching, it seems, was false: inflation *postpones* unemployment and exacerbates it; to remove unemployment inflation must *accelerate* until, perhaps, it destroys civilised society.

Why has the lesson been learned so late? Because economists are prone to fashion and text-books are slow to change? Because politicians found more votes in promises to abolish unemployment than to resist inflation? Because people in power apply the thinking – the 'ideas' – they learned as students? Perhaps the lesson would, nevertheless, have been learned earlier if 10 or 15 years of war and its aftermath of full employment siege economy had not precluded the lessons of Keynesian policies from being revealed in the late 1930s or 1940s.

The truth seems to be that, certainly in Britain, unemployment cannot in the end be avoided except by adapting the labour force to the changing requirements of world markets. For Britain, which exports some 20 per cent of its annual output, this truth is much more inconvenient than for America, which exports only some 5 per cent. Professor Laidler tentatively suggests that the 'natural' rate of unemployment for Britain may be about 2 per cent. If the unemployed find jobs on average in three months, 8 per cent of the labour force would change jobs each year. Even so, 2 per cent seems on the low side for the British economy, which must adapt its industry and labour force to unforeseen and unforeseeable changes in many and far-off countries over which she has little, or lessening, influence, or none. The old attitude was that unemployment was a tragedy; and so it was for many in the circumstances of 40 years ago. The new and hopeful attitude must be that unemployment is a necessary process in a changing economy, and that the role of the British government should be not to resist it by subsidising outdated industry and encouraging workers to believe that all jobs are for life, but to smooth the paths of change in general and to help individuals to adapt themselves to it.

Not least, this *Paper* shows, in both Professor Friedman's lecture and Professor Laidler's application to Britain, that analysis must precede decision, theory must inform practice, and, as always, ideas will determine action.

The Institute's constitution requires it to dissociate its Directors, Trustees and Advisers from the analysis and conclusions of economists whose work it sponsors (and publishes), but it commends Professor Friedman's lecture as the work of one of the world's most seminal and stimulating economic thinkers and its illumination of a *malaise* that has plagued Britain since the war and threatens to destroy her civilisation.

March 1975   ARTHUR SELDON

Milton Friedman

MILTON FRIEDMAN was born in 1912 in New York City and graduated from Rutgers before taking his MA at Chicago and PhD at Columbia. From 1935-37 he worked for the US National Resources Committee and from 1941-43 for the US Treasury.

Since 1946 Friedman has taught at the University of Chicago, where he is now the Paul Snowden Russell Distinguished Service Professor of Economics. He has taught also at the universities of Minnesota, Wisconsin, Columbia and California, as well as lecturing at universities throughout the world from Cambridge to Tokyo.

He is known to a wider audience as an advocate of a volunteer army (in place of the US draft), reverse income tax (in place of partial or universalist poverty programmes), monetary policy and floating exchange rates. He is the acknowledged head of the 'Chicago School' which specialises in the empirical testing of policy propositions derived from market analysis.

Among his best known books are *Essays in Positive Economics* (Chicago, 1953), *Studies in the Quantity Theory of Money* (edited by Friedman, Chicago, 1956), *A Theory of the Consumption Function* (Princeton, 1957), *Capitalism and Freedom* (Chicago, 1962), (with Anna J. Schwartz) *A Monetary History of the United States, 1867-1960* (Princeton, 1963), and *The Optimum Quantity of Money* (Aldine, Chicago, and Macmillan, London, 1969). The IEA has published his Wincott Memorial Lecture, *The Counter-Revolution in Monetary Theory* (Occasional Paper 33, 1970, 3rd impression 1974), *Monetary Correction* (Occasional Paper 41, 2nd impression 1974), and his contribution to *Inflation: Causes, Consequences, Cures* (IEA Readings No. 14, 1974, 2nd impression 1975).

David Laidler

DAVID E. W. LAIDLER was born in 1938 and educated at the London School of Economics, where he graduated BSc Econ with First Class Honours in 1959; the University of Syracuse (MA Economics, 1960);

[9]

and the University of Chicago (PhD, 1964). He has taught in both Britain (LSE, 1961-62; Lecturer in Economics, University of Essex, 1966-69) and the USA (Acting Professor, University of California, Berkeley, 1963-66; Acting Assistant Professor, Stanford University, Autumn 1964). He was appointed Professor of Economics at the University of Manchester in 1969. In 1971 he organised the History of Economic Thought Conference held at the University of Manchester to commemorate the centenary of the publication of W. S. Jevons's *Theory of Political Economy*; and he was the British Association for the Advancement of Science Lister Lecturer for 1972.

His publications include *The Demand for Money – Theories and Evidence* (International Textbook Co., 1969), and *Introduction to Microeconomics* (Philip Allan Publishers, 1974), and he edited (with David Purdy) *Labour Markets and Inflation* (Manchester University Press, 1974).

Unemployment versus Inflation?

An Evaluation of the Phillips Curve

MILTON FRIEDMAN

*Paul Snowden Russell Distinguished Service
Professor of Economics,
University of Chicago*

THE DISCUSSION of the Phillips curve started with truth in 1926, proceeded through error some 30 years later, and by now has returned back to 1926 and to the original truth. That is about 50 years for a complete circuit. You can see how technological development has speeded up the process of both producing and dissipating ignorance.

I

FISHER AND PHILLIPS

I CHOOSE the year 1926 not at random but because in that year Irving Fisher published an article in the *International Labour Review* under the title 'A Statistical Relation between Unemployment and Price Changes'.[1]

The Fisher approach
Fisher's article dealt with precisely the same empirical phenomenon that Professor A. W. Phillips analysed in his celebrated article in *Economica* some 32 years later.[2] Both were impressed with the empirical observation that inflation tended to be associated with low levels of unemployment and deflation with high levels. One amusing item in Fisher's article from a very different point of view is that he starts out by saying that he has been so deeply interested in this subject that 'during the last three years in particular I have had at

---

[1] June 1926, pp. 785-792. It was reprinted in the *Journal of Political Economy*, March/April, 1973, pp. 496-502.

[2] 'The Relation between Unemployment and the Rate of Change of Money Wage Rates in the United Kingdom, 1861-1957', *Economica*, November 1958, pp. 283-299.

[11]

least one computer in my office almost constantly at work on this project'.[1] Of course what he meant was a human being operating a calculating machine.

There was, however, a crucial difference between Fisher's analysis and Phillips', between the truth of 1926 and the error of 1958, which had to do with the direction of causation. Fisher took *the rate of change of prices* to be the independent variable that set the process going. In his words,

'When the dollar is losing value, or in other words when the price level is rising, a business man finds his receipts rising as fast, on the average, as this general rise of prices, but not his expenses, because his expenses consist, to a large extent, of things which are contractually fixed . . . Employment is then stimulated – for a time at least'.[2]

To elaborate his analysis and express it in more modern terms, let anything occur that produces a higher level of spending – or, more precisely, a higher rate of increase in spending than was anticipated. Producers would at first interpret the faster rate of increase in spending as an increase in real demand for their product. The producers of shoes, hats, or coats would discover that apparently there was an increase in the amount of goods they could sell at pre-existing prices. No one of them would know at first whether the change was affecting him in particular or whether it was general. In the first instance, each producer would be tempted to expand output, as Fisher states, and also to allow prices to rise. But at first much or most of the unanticipated increase in nominal demand (i.e. demand expressed in £s) would be absorbed by increases (or faster increases) in employment and output rather than by increases (or faster increases) in prices. Conversely, for whatever reason, let the rate of spending slow down, or rise less rapidly than was anticipated, and each individual producer would in the first instance interpret the slow-down at least partly as reflecting something peculiar to him. The result would be partly a slow-down in output and a rise in unemployment and partly a slow-down in prices.

Fisher was describing a *dynamic* process arising out of fluctuations in the rate of spending about some average trend or norm. He went

---

[1] Fisher, *op. cit.*, p. 786.
[2] *Ibid.*, p. 787.

out of his way to emphasise the importance of distinguishing between 'high and low prices on the one hand and the rise and fall
of prices on the other'.[1] He put it that way because he was writing
at a time when a stable level of prices was taken to be the norm.
Were he writing today, he would emphasise the distinction between
the rate of inflation and changes in the rate of inflation. (And perhaps some future writer will have to emphasise the difference between the second and the third derivatives!) The important
distinction – and it is quite clear that this is what Fisher had in mind –
is between *anticipated* and *unanticipated* changes.

The Phillips approach
Professor Phillips' approach was from exactly the opposite direction.

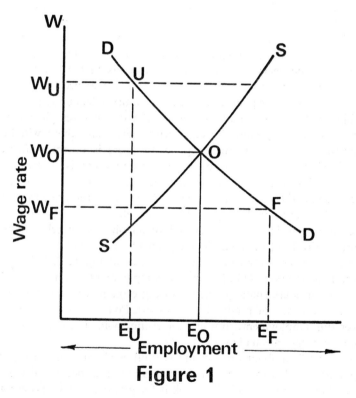

Figure 1

---

[1] *Ibid.*, p. 788.

[13]

He took the level of *employment* to be the independent variable that set the process going. He treated the rate of change of wages as the dependent variable. His argument was a very simple analysis – I hesitate to say simple-minded, but so it has proved – in terms of *static* supply and demand conditions. He said:

'When the demand for a commodity or service is high relatively to the supply of it we expect the price to rise, the rate of rise being greater the greater the excess demand . . . It seems plausible that this principle should operate as one of the factors determining the rate of change of money wage rates, which are the price of labour services'.[1]

Phillips' approach is based on the usual (*static*) demand and supply curves as illustrated in Figure 1. At the point of intersection, 0, the market is in equilibrium at the wage rate W_0, with the amount of labour employed E_0 equal to the amount of labour demanded. Unemployment is zero – which is to say, as measured, equal to 'frictional' or 'transitional' unemployment, or to use the terminology I adopted some years ago from Wicksell, at its 'natural' rate. At this point, says Phillips, there is no upward pressure on wages. Consider instead the point F, where the quantity of labour demanded is higher than the quantity supplied. There is over-employment, wages at W_F are below the equilibrium level, and there will be upward pressure on them. At point U, there is unemployment, W_U is above the equilibrium wage rate and there is downward pressure. The larger the discrepancy between the quantity of labour demanded and the quantity supplied, the stronger the pressure and hence the more rapidly wages will rise or fall.

Phillips translated this analysis into an observable relation by plotting the level of unemployment on one axis, and the rate of change of wages over time on the other, as in Figure 2. Point E_0 corresponds to point O in Figure 1. Unemployment is at its 'natural' rate so wages are stable (or in a growing economy, rising at a rate equal to the rate of productivity growth). Point F corresponds to 'over-full' employment, so wages are rising; point U to unemployment, so wages are falling.

Fisher talked about price changes, Phillips about wage changes, but I believe that for our purpose that is not an important distinction. Both Fisher and Phillips took it for granted that wages are a

[1] Phillips, *op. cit.*, p. 283.

[14]

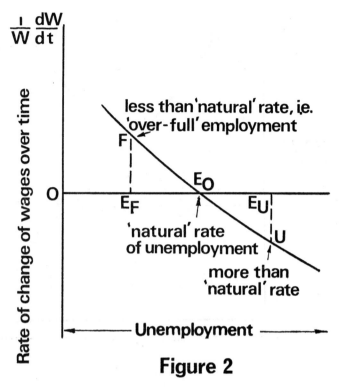

Figure 2

major component of total cost and that prices and wages would tend to move together. So both of them tended to go very readily from rates of wage change to rate of price change and I shall do so as well.

The fallacy in Phillips

Phillips' analysis seems very persuasive and obvious, yet it is utterly fallacious. It is fallacious because no economic theorist has ever asserted that the demand and supply of labour were functions of the *nominal* wage rate (i.e. wage rate expressed in £s). Every economic theorist from Adam Smith to the present would have told you that the vertical axis in Figure 1 should refer not to the *nominal* wage rate but to the *real* wage rate.

But once you label the vertical axis $\frac{W}{P}$ as in Figure 3, the graph has nothing to say about what is going to happen to *nominal wages* or prices. There is not even any *prima facie* presumption that it has

[15]

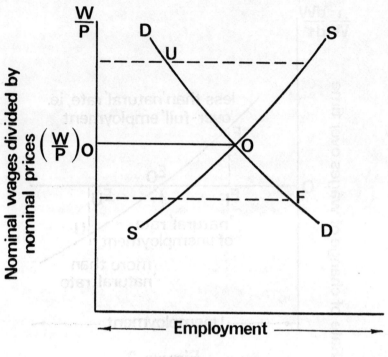

Figure 3

anything to say. For example, consider point 0 in Figure 3. At that level of employment, there is neither upward nor downward pressure on the real wage. But that real wage can remain constant with W and P separately *constant*, or with W and P each *rising* at the rate of 10 per cent a year, or *falling* at the rate of 10 per cent a year, or doing anything else, provided both change at the *same* rate.

II

THE KEYNESIAN CONFUSION BETWEEN
NOMINAL AND REAL WAGES

HOW DID a sophisticated mind like Phillips' – and he was certainly a highly sophisticated and subtle economist – come to confuse nominal wages with real wages ? He was led to do so by the general

[16]

intellectual climate that had been engendered by the Keynesian revolution. From this point of view, the essential element of the Keynesian revolution was the assumption that prices are highly rigid relative to output so that a change in demand of the kind considered by Fisher would be reflected almost entirely in *output* and very little in prices. The price level could be regarded as an institutional datum. The simple way to interpret Phillips is that he was therefore assuming the change in nominal wages to be equal to the change in real wages.

But that is not really what he was saying. What he was saying was slightly more sophisticated. It was that changes in *anticipated* nominal wages were equal to changes in *anticipated* real wages. There were two components of the Keynesian system that were essential to his construction: first, the notion that prices are rigid in the sense that people in planning their behaviour do not allow for the possibility that the price level might change, and hence regard a change in nominal wages or nominal prices as a change in real wages and real prices; second, that real wages *ex post* could be altered by *unanticipated* inflation. Indeed the whole Keynesian argument for the possibility of a full employment policy arose out of the supposition that it was possible to get workers (at least in the 1930s when Keynes wrote *The General Theory*) to accept lower real wages produced by inflation that they would not have accepted in the direct form of a reduction in nominal wages.[1]

These two components imply a sharp distinction between *anticipated* nominal and real wages and *actual* nominal and real wages. In the Keynesian climate of the time, it was natural for Phillips to take this distinction for granted, and to regard anticipated nominal and real wages as moving together.

I do not criticise Phillips for doing this. Science is possible only because at any one time there is a body of conventions or views or ideas that are taken for granted and on which scientists build. If

[1] J. M. Keynes, *The General Theory of Employment, Interest, and Money* (Macmillan, 1936): 'Whilst workers will usually resist a reduction of money-wages, it is not their practice to withdraw their labour whenever there is a rise in the price of wage-goods' (p. 9). ' . . . The workers, though unconsciously, are instinctively more reasonable economists than the classical school . . . They resist reductions of money-wages . . . whereas they do not resist reductions of real wages' (p. 14). ' . . . Since no trade union would dream of striking on every occasion of a rise in the cost of living, they do not raise the obstacle to any increase in aggregate employment attributed to them by the classical school' (p. 15).

each individual writer were to go back and question all the premises that underlie what he is doing, nobody would ever get anywhere. I believe that some of the people who have followed in his footsteps deserve much more criticism than he does for not noting the importance of this theoretical point once it was pointed out to them.

At any rate, it was this general intellectual climate that led Phillips to think in terms of nominal rather than real wages. The intellectual climate was also important in another direction. The Keynesian system, as everybody knows, is incomplete. It lacks an equation. A major reason for the prompt and rapid acceptance of the Phillips curve approach was the widespread belief that it provided the missing equation that connected the real system with the monetary system. In my opinion, this belief is false. What is needed to complete the Keynesian system is an equation that determines the equilibrium price level. But the Phillips curve deals with the relation between a rate of change of prices or wages and the level of unemployment. It does not determine an equilibrium price level. At any rate, the Phillips curve was widely accepted and was seized on immediately for policy purposes.[1] It is still widely used for this purpose as supposedly describing a 'trade-off', from a policy point of view, between inflation and unemployment.

It was said that what the Phillips curve means is that we are faced with a choice. If we choose a low level of inflation, say, stable prices, we shall have to reconcile ourselves to a high level of unemployment. If we choose a low level of unemployment, we shall have to reconcile ourselves to a high rate of inflation.

III

REACTION AGAINST THE KEYNESIAN SYSTEM

THREE DEVELOPMENTS came along in this historical account to change attitudes and to raise some questions.

One was the general theoretical reaction against the Keynesian

---

[1] For example, Albert Rees, 'The Phillips Curve as a Menu for Policy Choices', *Economica*, August 1970, pp. 227-238, explicitly considers the objections to a stable Phillips curve outlined below, yet concludes that there remains a trade-off that should be exploited. He writes: 'The strongest policy conclusion I can draw from the expectations literature is that the policy makers should not attempt to operate at a single point on the Phillips curve. . . . Rather, they should permit fluctuations in unemployment within a band' (p. 238).

system which brought out into the open the fallacy in the original Phillips curve approach of identifying nominal and real wages.

The second development was the failure of the Phillips curve relation to hold for other bodies of data. Fisher had found it to hold for the United States for the period before 1925; Phillips had found it to hold for Britain for a long period. But, lo and behold, when people tried it for any other place they never obtained good results. Nobody was able to construct a decent empirical Phillips curve for other circumstances. I may be exaggerating a bit – no doubt there are other successful cases; but certainly a large number of attempts were unsuccessful.

The third and most recent development is the emergence of 'stag-flation', which rendered somewhat ludicrous the confident statements that many economists had made about 'trade-offs', based on empirically-fitted Phillips curves.

Short- and long-run Phillips curves
The empirical failures and the theoretical reaction produced an attempt to rescue the Phillips curve approach by distinguishing a short-run from a long-run Phillips curve. Because both potential employers and potential employees envisage an implicit or explicit employment contract covering a fairly long period, both must guess in advance what real wage will correspond to a given nominal wage. Both therefore must form anticipations about the future price level. The real wage rate that is plotted on the vertical axis of the demand and supply curve diagram is thus not the *current* real wage but the *anticipated* real wage. If we suppose that anticipations about the price level are slow to change, while the nominal wage can change rapidly and is known with little time-lag, we can, for *short* periods, revert essentially to Phillips' original formulation, except that the equilibrium position is no longer a constant nominal wage, but a nominal wage changing at the same rate as the anticipated rate of change in prices (plus, for a growing economy, the anticipated rate of change in productivity). Changes in demand and supply will then show up first in a changed rate of change of nominal wages, which will mean also in anticipated real wages. Current prices may adjust as rapidly as or more rapidly than wages, so real wages *actually* received may move in the opposite direction from nominal wages, but *anticipated* real wages will move in the same direction.

[19]

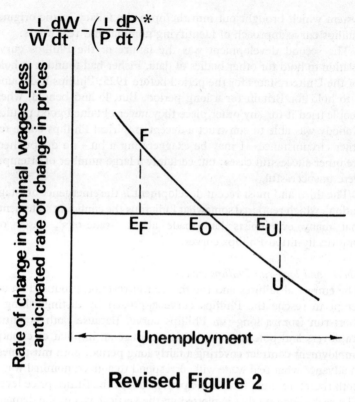

$$\frac{1}{W}\frac{dW}{dt} - \left(\frac{1}{P}\frac{dP}{dt}\right)^{\!\!*}$$

Rate of change in nominal wages less anticipated rate of change in prices

F

O

E_F E_O E_U

U

◄———— Unemployment ————►

Revised Figure 2

One way to put this in terms of the Phillips curve is to plot on the vertical axis not the change in nominal wages but that change minus the anticipated rate of change in prices, as in the revised Figure 2, where $\left(\frac{1}{P}\frac{dP}{dt}\right)^{\!\!*}$, standing for the anticipated rate of change in prices, is subtracted from $\frac{1}{W}\frac{dW}{dt}$. This curve now tells a story much more like Fisher's original story than Phillips'. Suppose, to start with, the economy is at point E_0, with both prices and wages stable (abstracting from growth). Suppose something, say, a monetary expansion, starts nominal aggregate demand growing, which in turn produces a rise in prices and wages at the rate of, say, 2 per cent per year. Workers will initially interpret this as a rise in their real wage – because they still anticipate constant prices – and so will be willing to offer more labour (move up their supply curve), i.e. employment grows and unemployment falls. Employers may have

[20]

the same anticipations as workers about the general price level, but they are more directly concerned about the price of the products they are producing and far better informed about that. They will initially interpret a rise in the demand for and price of their product as a rise in its relative price and as implying a fall in the real wage rate they must pay measured in terms of their product. They will therefore be willing to hire more labour (move down their demand curve). The combined result is a movement, say, to point F, which corresponds with 'over-full' employment, with nominal wages rising at 2 per cent per year.

But, as time passes, both employers and employees come to recognise that prices *in general* are rising. As Abraham Lincoln said, you can fool all of the people some of the time, you can fool some of the people all of the time, but you can't fool all of the people all of the time. As a result, they raise their estimate of the anticipated rate of inflation, which reduces the rate of rise of anticipated real wages, and leads you to slide down the curve back ultimately to the point E_0. There is thus a *short-run* 'trade-off' between inflation and unemployment, but *no long-run* 'trade-off'.

By incorporating price anticipations into the Phillips curve as I have just done, I have implicitly begged one of the main issues in the recent controversy about the Phillips curve. Thanks to recent experience of 'stagflation' plus theoretical analysis, everyone now admits that the apparent short-run Phillips curve is misleading and seriously overstates the *short*-run trade-off, but many are not willing to accept the view that the *long*-run trade-off is *zero*.

We can examine this issue by using a different way of incorporating price anticipations into the Phillips curve. Figure 4 keeps the rate of change of nominal wages on the vertical axis but contains a series of different curves, one for each anticipated rate of growth of wages. To put it algebraically, instead of writing the Phillips curve relation as

(1) $$\frac{1}{W}\frac{dW}{dt} - \left(\frac{1}{P}\frac{dP}{dt}\right)^{\star} = f(U),$$

where U is unemployment, we can write it in more general form as

(2) $$\frac{1}{W}\frac{dW}{dt} = f\left[U, \left(\frac{1}{P}\frac{dP}{dt}\right)^{\star}\right].$$

Now suppose something occurs to put the economy at point F at which wages are rising at 2 per cent a year and unemployment is

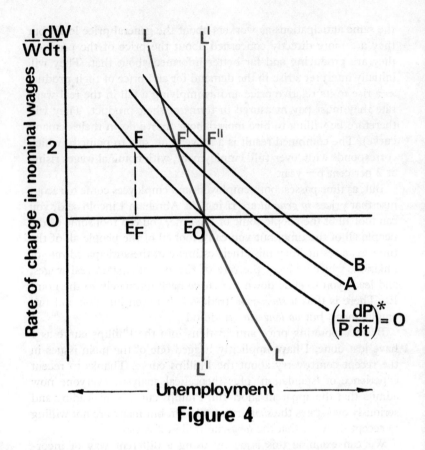

Figure 4

less than the natural rate. Then, as people adjust their expectations of inflation, the short-run Phillips curve will shift upwards and the final resting place would be on that short-run Phillips curve at which the anticipated rate of inflation equals the current rate. The issue now becomes whether that Phillips curve is like A, so that the long-run curve is negatively sloping, like LL, in which case an anticipated rate of inflation of 2 per cent will still reduce the level of unemployment, though not by as much as an unanticipated rate of 2 per cent, or whether it is like B, so that the long-run curve is *vertical*, that is, unemployment is the *same* at a 2 per cent anticipated rate of inflation as at a zero per cent anticipated rate.

[22]

IV

No LONG-RUN MONEY ILLUSION

IN MY Presidential Address to the American Economic Association
seven years ago, I argued that the long-run Phillips curve was
vertical, largely on the grounds I have already sketched here: in
effect, the absence of any long-run money illusion.[1] At about the
same time, Professor E. S. Phelps, now of Columbia University,
offered the same hypothesis, on different though related grounds.[2]
This hypothesis has come to be called the 'accelerationist' hypothesis or the 'natural rate' hypothesis. It has been called accelerationist because a policy of trying to hold unemployment below the
horizontal intercept of the long-run vertical Phillips curve must lead
to an *accelerated* inflation.

Suppose, beginning at point E_0 on Figure 4, when nobody anticipated any inflation, it is decided to aim at a lower unemployment
level, say E_F. This can be done initially by producing an inflation
of 2 per cent, as shown by moving along the Phillips curve corresponding to anticipations of no inflation. But, as we have seen, the
economy will not stay at F because people's anticipations will shift,
and if the rate of inflation were kept at 2 per cent, the economy
would be driven back to the level of unemployment it started with.
The only way unemployment can be kept below the 'natural rate'
is by an *ever-accelerating* inflation, which always keeps current inflation ahead of anticipated inflation. Any resemblance between that
analysis and what you in Britain have been observing in practice is
not coincidental: what recent British governments have tried to do
is to keep unemployment below the natural rate, and to do so they
have had to accelerate inflation – from 3.9 per cent in 1964 to 16.0 per
cent in 1974, according to your official statistics.[3]

Misunderstandings about the 'natural rate' of unemployment
The hypothesis came to be termed the 'natural rate' hypothesis

[1] 'The Role of Monetary Policy', *American Economic Review*, March 1968,
pp. 1-17.

[2] 'Money Wage Dynamics and Labour Market Equilibrium,' in E. S. Phelps
(ed.), *Microeconomic Foundations of Employment and Inflation Theory*, Norton
Press, New York, 1970.

[3] United Kingdom General Index of Retail Prices, *Department of Employment
Gazette*.

because of the emphasis on the natural rate of unemployment. The term 'the natural rate' has been misunderstood. It does not refer to some *irreducible minimum* of unemployment. It refers rather to that rate of employment which is consistent with the *existing real conditions* in the labour market. It can be lowered by removing obstacles in the labour market, by reducing friction. It can be raised by introducing additional obstacles. The purpose of the concept is to separate the monetary from the non-monetary aspects of the employment situation – precisely the same purpose that Wicksell had in using the word 'natural' in connection with the rate of interest.

In the past few years, a large number of statistical studies have investigated the question whether the long-run Phillips curve is or is not vertical. That dispute is still in train.

Most of the statistical tests were undertaken by rewriting Equation (2) in the form:

$$(3) \qquad \frac{1}{W} \frac{dW}{dt} = a + b\left(\frac{1}{P} \frac{dP}{dt}\right)^* + f(U)$$

or

$$\frac{1}{P} \frac{dP}{dt} = a + b\left(\frac{1}{P} \frac{dP}{dt}\right)^* + f(U),$$

where the left-hand side was either the rate of change of wages or the rate of change of prices. The question then asked was the value of b.[1] The original Phillips curve essentially assumed $b=0$; the acceleration hypothesis set b equal to 1. The authors of the various tests I am referring to used observed data, mostly time-series data, to estimate the numerical value of b.[2] Almost every such test has come out with a numerical value of b less than 1, implying

---

[1] This is the coefficient of the anticipated rate of inflation, that is, the percentage point change in the current rate of change in wages or in prices that would result from a 1 percentage point change in the anticipated rate of inflation.

[2] I might note as an aside that one much noticed attempt along these lines was contained in lectures given in Britain by Robert Solow a few years ago (*Price Expectations and the Behaviour of the Price Level*, Manchester University Press, 1969). Unfortunately, his test has a fatal flaw which renders it irrelevant to the current issue. In order to allow for costs as well as demand, he included on the right-hand side of an equation like Equation (3) the rate of change of wages, and, on the left-hand side, the rate of change of prices. In such an equation, there is no reason to expect b to be unity even on the strictest acceleration hypothesis, because the equation is then an equation to determine what happens to the margin between prices and wages. Let the anticipated rate of inflation rise by one percentage point, but the rate of change of wages be held constant, and any resulting rise in prices raises the excess of prices over costs and so stimulates output. Hence, in Solow's equation, the strict acceleration hypothesis would imply that b was less than 1.

that there is a long-run 'trade-off'.[1] However, there are a number of difficulties with these tests, some on a rather superficial level, others on a much more fundamental level.

One obvious statistical problem is that the statistically fitted curves have not been the same for different periods of fit and have produced very unreliable extrapolations for periods subsequent to the period of fit. So it looks very much as if the statistical results are really measuring a *short*-term relationship despite the objective. The key problem here is that, in order to make the statistical test, it is necessary to have some measure of the anticipated rate of inflation. Hence, every such test is a joint test of the accelerationist hypothesis and a particular hypothesis about the formation of anticipations.

V

THE ADAPTIVE EXPECTATIONS HYPOTHESIS

MOST OF these statistical tests embody the so-called adaptive expectations hypothesis, which has worked well in many problems. It states that anticipations are revised on the basis of the difference between the current rate of inflation and the anticipated rate. If the anticipated rate was, say, 5 per cent but the current rate 10 per cent, the anticipated rate will be revised upward by some fraction of the difference between 10 and 5. As is well known, this implies that the anticipated rate of inflation is an exponentially weighted average of past rates of inflation, the weights declining as one goes back in time.

Even on their own terms, then, these results are capable of two different interpretations. One is that the long-run Phillips curve is not vertical but has a negative slope. The other is that this has not been a satisfactory method of evaluating people's expectations for this purpose.

A somewhat more subtle statistical problem with these equations is that, if the accelerationist hypothesis is correct, the results are either estimates of a short-run curve or are statistically unstable. Suppose the true value of b is unity. Then when current inflation equals anticipated inflation, which is the definition of a long-run curve, we have that

(4) $f(U) = -a.$

[1] A succinct summary of these studies is in S. J. Turnovsky, 'On the Role of Inflationary Expectations in a Short-Run Macro-Economic Model', *Economic Journal*, June 1974, pp. 317-337, especially pp. 326-327.

This is the vertical long-run Phillips curve with the value of U that satisfies it being the natural rate of unemployment. Any other values of U reflect either short-term equilibrium positions or a stochastic component in the natural rate. But the estimation process used, with $\frac{1}{P}\frac{dP}{dt}$ on the left-hand side, treats different observed rates of unemployment as if they were exogenous, as if they could persist indefinitely. There is simply no way of deriving Equation (4) from such an approach. In effect, the implicit assumption that unemployment can take different values begs the whole question raised by the accelerationist hypothesis. On a statistical level, this approach requires putting U, or a function of U, on the left-hand side, not $\frac{1}{P}\frac{dP}{dt}$.

VI

RATIONAL EXPECTATIONS

A STILL MORE fundamental criticism has recently been made by a number of economists in the United States. This criticism has its origin in an important article by John Muth on rational expectations. The rational expectations approach has been applied to the problem in recent articles by Robert Lucas of Carnegie-Mellon (now of Chicago), Tom Sargent of the University of Minnesota, and a number of others.[1]

This criticism is that you cannot take seriously the notion that people form anticipations on the basis of a weighted average of past experience with fixed weights – or any other scheme that is inconsistent with the way inflation is really being generated. For example, let us suppose that the current course of the price level is the one drawn on panel A of Figure 5, that inflation is accelerating. With a

---

[1] John Muth, 'Rational Expectations and the Theory of Price Movements', *Econometrica*, July 1961, pp. 315-335; Robert E. Lucas, 'Econometric Testing of the Natural Rate Hypothesis', in Otto Eckstein (ed.), *The Econometrics of Price Determination Conference*, Board of Governors of the Federal Reserve System and Social Science Research Council, Washington, 1972, 'Econometric Policy Evaluation: A Critique', Carnegie-Mellon University Working Paper, 1973, 'Some International Evidence on Output-Inflation Tradeoffs', *American Economic Review*, June 1973, pp. 326-334; Thomas J. Sargent, 'Rational Expectations, the Real Rate of Interest, and the "Natural" Rate of Unemployment', *Brookings Papers on Economic Activity*, Vol. 2, 1973, pp. 429-472; and Thomas J. Sargent and Neil Wallace, ' "Rational" Expectations, the Optimal Money Instrument and the Optimal Money Supply Rule', *Journal of Political Economy*, April 1974.

[26]

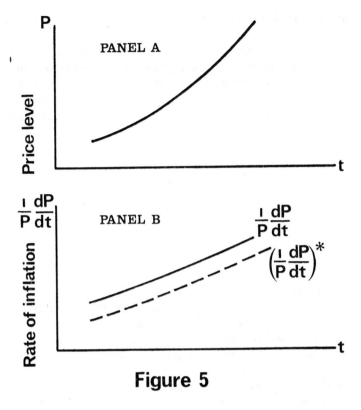

Figure 5

fixed exponential weighting pattern (with weights summing to unity) the anticipated rate of inflation will always be lagging behind, as in Panel B. But people who are forming anticipations are not fools – or at least some of them are not. They are not going to *persist* in being wrong. And more generally they are not going to base their anticipations solely on the past history of prices. Is there anybody in this room whose anticipation of inflation next year will be independent of the result of the coming British elections ? That is not reported in the past record of prices. Will it be independent of policies announced by the parties that come into power, and so on ? Therefore, said Muth, we should assume that people form their anticipations on the basis of a correct economic theory: not that they are right in *each individual* case but that over any long period they will *on the average* be right. Sometimes this will lead to the formation

[27]

of anticipations on the basis of adaptive expectations, but by no means always.

If you apply that idea to the present problem it turns out that, if the true world is one in which people form expectations on a rational basis so that on the average they are right, then assuming that they form expectations by averaging the past with fixed weights will yield a value of b in equation (3) less than unity even though the true value is unity.

Consider a world in which there is a vertical long-run Phillips curve and in which people form their expectations rationally, so that on the average, over a long period, their expectations are equal to what happens. In such a world, the statistician comes along and estimates equation (3) on the assumption that people form their anticipations by averaging past experience with fixed weights. What will he find? It turns out that he will find that b is less than 1. Of course, this possibility does not prove that the statistical tests incorporating adaptive expectations are wrong but only provides an alternative interpretation of their results.

In a series of very interesting and important papers, Lucas and Sargent[1] have explored the implication of the rational expectations hypothesis and have tried to derive empirical tests of the slope of the long-run Phillips curve without the possibly misleading assumption of adaptive expectations.

Their empirical tests use a different kind of information. For example, one implication of a rational expectations hypothesis is that, in a country in which prices have fluctuated a great deal, expectations will respond to changes in the current rate of inflation much more rapidly than in a country in which prices have been relatively stable. It follows that the observed short-run Phillips curve will be steeper in the first country than in the second. Comparisons among countries in this way, as well as other tests, seem so far entirely consistent with what any reasonable man must surely expect: which is that, *since you can't fool all the people all the time, the true long-run Phillips curve is vertical.*

[1] Footnote 1, p. 26.

VII

IMPLICATIONS FOR THEORY AND POLICY

THE EVIDENCE is by no means all in. Some of the articles I have referred to are not yet published and some have been published only in the past two or three years. So we certainly cannot regard the matter as settled. Even so, it is worth noting how far-reaching are the implications of this view not only for the Phillips curve problem but also for policy.

One very strong and very important implication for policy is that, if you treat people as forming expectations on a rational basis, no fixed rule of monetary or fiscal policy will enable you to achieve anything other than the natural rate of unemployment. And you can see why. Because – to go back to my initial Phillips curve analysis – the only way in which you ever get a reduction of unemployment is through *unanticipated* inflation.

If the government follows any fixed rule whatsoever, *so long as the people know it,* they will be able to take it into account. And consequently you cannot achieve an unemployment target other than the natural rate by any fixed rule. The only way you can do so is by continually being cleverer than all the people, by continually making up *new* rules and using them for a while until people catch up on them. Then you must invent a new set of rules. That is not a very promising possibility.

This analysis provides a different sort of intellectual background for a view that some of us have held for a long time: that it is a better approach to policy to say that you are going to co-operate with the people and inform them of what you are doing, so giving them a basis for their judgements, rather than trying to fool them. What the Sargent/Lucas argument and analysis really suggests is that you are fooling yourself if you think that you can fool them.

That is about where the present state of the argument is. I might summarise by saying that there is essentially no economist any longer who believes in the naive Phillips curve of the kind originally proposed. The argument has shifted now to a second level, where everybody agrees that the long-run Phillips curve is steeper than the short-run Phillips curve. The only argument is whether it is vertical or not quite so vertical. And here the evidence is not quite all in. But there is a line of approach in analysis and reasoning which enables you to interpret, so far as I know, all the existing evidence consistently on the hypothesis of a long-run vertical Phillips curve.

ADDENDUM

QUESTIONS AND ANSWERS ON

THE TRADE UNIONS AND INFLATION

LORD (WILFRED) BROWN: Can one leave trade union power out of account in all these equations?

PROFESSOR FRIEDMAN: I will quote from another famous American writer, a humorist and not an economist, who said, 'The trouble with people ain't ignorance, it's what they know that ain't so'. Trade unions play a very important role in determining the position of the natural level of unemployment. They play a more important role in denying opportunities to some classes in the community that are open to others. They play a very important role in the structure of the labour force and the structure of *relative* wages. But, despite appearances to the contrary, a *given* amount of trade union power does not play any role in exacerbating inflation. It is true that if relatively weak unions become strong, *in the process of going from weak to strong* they may exert an interim inflationary influence. They will, in the process, drive up the real wages of their members. This will reduce the level of employment in their sector. Insofar as the government has a full employment policy and is sensitive to the total level of unemployment, it will adopt expansionary policies and drive up the level of money demand. This is capable of producing a *temporary* rise to a new level of prices. But it does not produce continuing inflation. The strong union will then get its new real wage rate, and there will be a re-alignment of employment in the various industries.

What seems so obvious ought to be judged against a broader range of experience. If A produces B, then where you have A you should have B. If A is the only factor that produces B, then where you have B you should have A. If you look around the world and at your own (British) experience, and our (American) experience, you will find there are many periods when you had strong unions and there was no inflation. There are many periods when you had no unions and a great deal of inflation. Historically there simply is nothing like a one-to-one relationship between strong trade unions and inflation. Let me explain the fallacy in the argument as I see it. I think you will agree that strong industrial monopolies do not produce inflation; they produce high relative prices for the products they are monopolising, and low output for those products. If a monopoly gets stronger, or if a monopoly replaces competition, in the process of going from competition to monopoly, it will drive up the relative price of its product and reduce the output. If there is difficulty in absorbing the redundant employees created in that way, once again there may be a once-for-all rise in the price level, but there is no *continuous* process of inflation.

Why are unions different? People say, because unions are not maximising profit. But that is not really relevant. Union behaviour is not an utterly random, erratic thing; it is determined by some objectives, whatever they may be. The question you must ask is: Is there an equilibrium real wage? Analysis of that problem shows the fallacy in the more sophisticated arguments that propose to demonstrate unions' responsibility for inflation.

Suppose that all union agreements run for three years, and that, whenever they are negotiated, they include a provision for a 100 per cent cost-of-living adjustment. Then unions are truly negotiating for real wages. How can strong unions under those circumstances create inflation? There is no way. A strong union can create social conflict, it can drive people out of work, it can create unemployment. If it becomes stronger, and therefore the number of people employed in its areas is going to be smaller as it is driving up its real wage, it can create temporary inflation in the process because of some policy which is absorbing the unemployed without a wage decrease. But it cannot create *continuing* inflation.

I may say I am absolutely appalled by the widespread belief I find in Britain that you can use the paper club of price and wage control to beat down the rigid power of trade unions, that you can do by subterfuge and in indirect ways what you are not prepared to do directly and openly.

MARK BRADY: What is the possibility that a process of inflation, by producing a misallocation of resources and malinvestment, will raise the natural rate of unemployment so that the Phillips curve will be bent to the *right* rather than be vertical?

[31]

PROFESSOR FRIEDMAN: That is a very difficult question to answer. The crucial problem arises whether the inflation is open or repressed. If the inflation is open – if there are no restrictions – there is no reason why it should produce malinvestment. It will produce a maldistribution of resources by inducing people to hold smaller cash balances than they otherwise would, by inducing them to waste resources in doing physically what could be done with the aid of money. That would make the level of *real income* lower than it otherwise would be, but there is no reason why it should alter the level of employment or unemployment. That is a different question.

In order to determine the effect on *employment* you would have to know whether the activities that are substituted for money operate in a labour market with different frictional characteristics from those in other industries.

Similarly, it is not clear what will happen to the rate of growth. The level of output will always be lower with high inflation than with low inflation, but that does not mean that output may not be growing at the same rate.

In practice, inflation is not likely to be open. In my opinion far more harm is done by the measures which are taken to repress inflation than is done by the open inflation itself. Consequently, if you are realistically going to consider different rates of inflation, then I believe that what you are saying is correct, not because of the inflation, but because the higher the rate of inflation the more widespread is likely to be the government interference in the market. In effect, such interference is equivalent to increasing the amount of frictions and obstacles in the labour market, and therefore does tend to create a higher level of unemployment. That is why, when reporters and others ask how much unemployment it will cost to reduce inflation, I say to them, when did you last beat your wife? How much unemployment will it cost *not* to beat inflation?

You must not let yourself be carried away by the naive Phillips curve approach and suppose that there really is a trade-off here. Given the way in which the political and economic structure will adapt itself to different rates of inflation, *if you continue to let inflation accelerate you are going to have higher unemployment either way*. So you only have a choice between which way you want the unemployment to come. Do you want it to come while you are getting sicker or do you want it to come while you are getting better?

[32]

QUESTION (speaker's identity unknown): How do you reconcile the following situation with what you have just said? Supposing you have a situation with a firm or industry employing, say, 20,000 people, and unions are pressing up the wages. And then government controls the price at which the product is being sold. There comes a point where the firm says to the government: 'We cannot produce this any more, give us a subsidy'. Is not that inflation because of falling production and/or more money being pushed around?

PROFESSOR FRIEDMAN: The subsidy itself is not inflation. If the subsidy is financed by printing money the consequence will be inflation. If the subsidy is financed by taxing somebody else to pay the subsidy there is no inflation.

I am not saying that the existence of strong unions may not be one of the factors that, by a variety of devices, affects what monetary policy is. But in this respect it is just one of many influences. What produces the inflation is not trade unions, nor monopolistic employers, but what happens to the quantity of money. Anything else *that affects the quantity of money* will have the same effect.

Moreover, I go further. I can speak more confidently of my own country than I can of yours. In my country the theoretical possibilities we have discussed here – that union-caused unemployment would produce reactions on the part of governments which would promote inflation – have *not* empirically been the source of inflation. In the US the experience is that union wages have tended to lag *behind* inflation rather than to precede it. Almost all union confrontations have been 'catch-ups'. Unions have been blamed for inflation for the same reason that in this country your government blames the price of oil for inflation. Every government looks for scapegoats for its own deficiencies. That is what has happened in my country. It is what has happened in Britain.

I doubt that, in practice, any large part of your inflationary problem has been produced by mischievous unions. No doubt there have been many mischievous actions; I am not saying there have not. I am not trying to defend unions, far from it. I think they do an enormous amount of harm. But I believe that we do no good by using bad reasons for good objectives. We ought to face up to the problem of the correct policy about unions, on the relevant grounds that unions deny people opportunities to employ their resources in the most effective way and keep the standard of life of the ordinary people of Britain lower than it otherwise would be, but not on the utterly false and irrelevant grounds that in some way they are manufacturers of money and of inflation.

We must not suppose we are dealing with a completely new phenomenon. Inflations have been with us for two thousand years. The inflation in Diocletian's time was not produced by strong trade unions! Nor were almost any of the other historical inflations.

In your country and in mine, every businessman is persuaded that inflation is produced by labour unions, or by wage pressure, whether or not from trade unions. And that is because of the fallacy of composition. What is true for each individual is often the *opposite* of what is true for everybody together. Any person in this room could get out of that door in two seconds; but if everybody tried at once to get out of that door, you could not do it. In the same way, pressure on an employer to increase his prices comes to him in the form of an increase in wages and costs. It looks to him as if he is being required to increase prices because of that increase in wages and costs. That is true for him by himself. But where did that increase in costs come from? It came because somewhere else in the system somebody was increasing demand, which was tending to draw away the employer's labour or other resources. He was required to bid in the market to keep them.

In *University Economics*,[1] Professors A. A. Alchian and W. R. Allen have an excellent little parable which I think brings this truth home very well. It says, let us suppose in a country in which everything else is fine all of a sudden there is a great craze for increasing the consumption of meat, and all the housewives rush to the butchers to buy meat. The butchers are delighted to sell them the meat. They do not mark up the prices at all, they just sell out all the meat they have, but they place additional orders with the wholesalers. The wholesalers are delighted to sell the meat. They clean out their inventories. They go back to the packing houses. The packing houses ship out their meat. The price is the same but the packing houses send orders to their buyers at the cattle market: 'Buy more beef'. There is only a fixed amount of cattle available.

[1] 3rd edn., Wadsworth Publishing Co., Belmont, California, 1972; international paperback edn., with a new Introduction by A. J. Culyer, Prentice-Hall, Hemel Hempstead, Herts., 1974, pp. 95-97.

And so the only thing that happens is that in the process of each packer trying to buy more beef he bids up the price. Then a notice goes from the packer to the wholesaler, 'We are very sorry, but due to an increase in our costs we are required to increase the price'. A notice goes from the wholesaler to the retailer. And the retailer finally says to the customer when she comes in to complain that beef has gone up, 'I'm terribly sorry, but my *costs* have gone up'. He's right. But what started the increase in costs all the way up and down the line? It was the *housewife* rushing in to buy the meat.

In exactly the same way, every businessman has a misconception of the process. From his point of view he is right – the pressure on him to raise his prices derives from increases in costs. If there happen to be unions, he will attribute it to the pressure of the unions. If there are no unions, he will attribute it to some other force which is driving up wages – perhaps the world shortage of sugar, or the Arabs. But the truth of the matter is that the ultimate source of inflation is always that increase in *demand* which percolates through to him in this or some other form.

The End of 'Demand Management': How to Reduce Unemployment in the 1970s

DAVID E. W. LAIDLER
Professor of Economics,
University of Manchester

I

THE DEBATE ON MONEY AND INFLATION

THE 'KEYNESIAN-MONETARIST' debate was originally about the importance of the quantity of money as an influence on the level of aggregate demand. The majority of professional economists now regard the broad outlines of that debate as settled for the moment by the enormous amount of empirical evidence [1]* which research over the last two decades has generated. The quantity of money is an important variable, though not all-important, and only relatively small groups of extremists, such as some British Keynesians,[2] who unfortunately still exercise an important influence on policy in Britain, refuse to recognise this truth.

The focus of professional debate has now shifted to the effect of variations in aggregate demand on the rate of inflation. On the monetarist side it is believed that the inter-relationship is strong enough to permit the current inflation, both in Britain and elsewhere, to be dealt with, though not without costs, by orthodox restrictive fiscal and monetary policies. On the Keynesian side, particularly in Britain, it is believed that, though such policies will affect the level of income and employment, they will have no effect on the rate of inflation, which, say the Keynesians, is determined by wage-

---

[1] For a survey of this evidence, see Laidler [1971a].
[2] For example, see Kaldor [1970].
* See References, pp. 47-48.

push factors that operate independently of aggregate demand, as well as by the behaviour of the world prices of commodity imports and of the exchange rate. Professor Friedman's IEA Lecture is a contribution to the monetarist side of the debate. He gives a lucid account of the theoretical framework which underpins the 'monetarist' views on these matters and a brief survey of the state of the empirical debate in the United States. I will be mainly concerned with the implications of the ideas for our understanding of the British economy.

II

'DEMAND MANAGEMENT' IN THE 1960s
BASED ON THE PHILLIPS CURVE

IT WAS widely believed in this country during the 1960s that there existed an extremely simple and stable inverse relationship between the level of unemployment and the rate of wage and price inflation, a relationship known as the 'Phillips curve'. Since it was thought that unemployment could be varied by government policy on the level of aggregate demand ('demand management'), policy on inflation was thought to be straightforward. A little more unemployment would produce a little less inflation, and, if price stability was what was desired, an unemployment rate of about 2½ per cent would do the trick.

This simple 'Phillips curve' relationship has, of course, been completely discredited by experience since 1969, but it came under strong theoretical attack before then both from Professor Friedman [1968] and Professor Phelps [1967].[1] The Phillips curve was based on the proposition that the *money* wage level would rise when demand for labour was high relatively to supply (and hence unemployment low). Friedman and Phelps argued, with complete justification, that simple economic theory said the relevant wage variable for this proposition was the *real* wage rate (the money wage rate adjusted for variations in the general price level), not the money wage rate alone. To those of us who had read and understood their work, the behaviour of price and wage inflation rates after 1969

[1] The theoretical arguments of Friedman and Phelps are not identical but they reach the same conclusions by their somewhat different routes. The discussion that follows is closer to Friedman's approach than to Phelps's.

[37]

came as no surprise. Not only did they criticise existing theory about the interaction between inflation and unemployment; they proposed an alternative explanation which, qualitatively at least, seems to conform reasonably well to recent experience, both in Britain and the United States.

III

THE NEW EXPLANATION OF INFLATION

(A) Inflation Rate and Aggregate Demand

THIS ALTERNATIVE theory has three components. First, it states that firms, in setting a time-path for their prices, and in bargaining with the labour force over the time-path of money wages, take their *expectations* of the future rate of inflation into account, as do members of the labour force, whether unionised or not, when they decide on the wage offers they are willing to accept. Thus, if a 10 per cent inflation rate is expected to prevail, firms will plan to raise the price of their output at that same rate, while money wages will rise at a rate 10 percentage points higher than they would if a zero inflation rate was anticipated. If all firms make their decisions this way, and if their ability to sell their output and hire labour turns out in practice to be what they expected, they will have no incentive to alter their initial pricing plans and wage agreements. The price inflation rate will indeed turn out to be 10 per cent as a result of what amounts to a self-fulfilling prophecy. But if firms find they cannot sell all they want to sell, if they run into deficient demand for their output, and if they find that, given the wages they are offering, they can hire more labour than they want, they will revise their prices and their wages downwards relatively to initial plans. Thus, in the face of deficient aggregate demand the general inflation rate will be lower than expected. By exactly parallel reasoning, excess aggregate demand will lead to inflation rising above the rate initially expected. Thus the first component of the new theory is the proposition that the inflation rate varies, *relatively to the expected inflation rate*, with the level of aggregate demand in the economy.

(B) 'Natural' Rate of Unemployment independent of the Inflation Rate

Its second component is the so-called 'natural unemployment rate hypothesis', which states that there is a unique amount of unemployment corresponding to the aggregate demand at which the inflation rate neither accelerates nor slows down relatively to expectations. What determines this unique amount of unemployment will be touched on below (pp. 44-45). The important point is that it is supposed to be completely *independent* of the expected rate of inflation. Hence in the long run the unemployment-inflation 'trade-off' vanishes, and the Phillips curve becomes *vertical*.

Now if there were independent observations on the expected rate of inflation it would be easy to put these propositions to the test and discover whether indeed there was a particular amount of unemployment which, if exceeded, led to the inflation rate falling below the expected rate, or, if it fell short, led to the inflation rate rising above the expected rate. Unfortunately independent observations on expectations are not easy to come by. This difficulty forces one to add a third component to the Friedman/Phelps theory before it can be subjected to test, namely an hypothesis that will enable us to deduce the value of the expected rate of inflation from readily observable variables.

(C) The Error-Learning Hypothesis
One appealing and widely used approach to this problem is to propose that the expected rate of inflation at any moment will depend upon the past behaviour of the inflation rate. The 'error-learning' (or 'adaptive expectations', the terms are synonymous) hypothesis dealt with in detail by Professor Friedman (Lecture, p. 25) represents a specific form of precisely this approach. It proposes that expectations are formed period by period (year by year, say) by taking the expectation at the beginning of a period, comparing it to what happens (i.e. observing the error) and revising expectations for the next period in proportion to the size of the error (i.e. learning from the error and thereby adapting the expectation). Mathematically this procedure turns out to be equivalent to treating the expected inflation rate as given by a weighted average of all past inflation rates, the weights declining geometrically as one goes into the past, and adding up to one.

The adoption of the error-learning explanation 'solves' in a formal sense the difficulty in observing what people expect. But, like the natural unemployment rate hypothesis, or the hypothesis that

[39]

variations in aggregate demand affect the inflation rate, it could be wrong. It solves one problem only at the cost of creating another. When we compare predictions of this new theory with empirical evidence, all is well and good if all the predictions conform to observations; but if they do not it would be helpful to know which component of the theory is wrong. In this event, as Professor Friedman shows (pp. 25-26), the structure of the theory does not permit us to find out. Although there is abundant evidence consistent with the proposition that the inflation rate does respond systematically to aggregate demand (or unemployment), given expectations, and showing that the past rate of inflation does exert an important influence on the expected rate, only some of the evidence is consistent simultaneously with the proposition that it does so in accordance with a strict error-learning mechanism and with the natural unemployment rate explanation. This seems to be true of the United States economy, or the British. But before going into the likely source of these difficulties, or the reasons why it is important that they be solved, I shall say a little about the policy implications of the positive results that have been achieved.[1]

IV

EXPECTATIONS CHANGE OVER TIME

THE ORIGINAL, over-simple Phillips curve suggested that, by restricting demand, government created extra unemployment and lowered the inflation rate, both consequences being permanent. Even if we do not stick to the natural unemployment rate hypothesis but consider only the implications of propositions on which the evidence is far more clear-cut, the new theory tells us that, when demand is restricted, unemployment will increase and the inflation rate will fall. But it also tells us to regard these events as only the first step in a dynamic process whose effects are spread out over

[1] Professor Friedman notes at the end of his Lecture that there is less disagreement among economists on a short-run trade-off between inflation and unemployment that becomes less acute with the passage of time than on whether the trade-off ultimately vanishes altogether. However, among British economists the view that the inflation is independent of excess demand is much more widespread than it seems to be in America. Professor Sir John Hicks [1974], Chapter 5, contains an account of this view. In the light of available evidence I find it hard to see how it can be maintained.

time. With the passage of time a lower inflation rate will cause inflationary expectations to be revised downwards; hence there will be a further fall in the inflation rate even if policy is such as to maintain unemployment at the same level as before. Alternatively, it is possible to think of policy being arranged so as to hold the inflation rate at its new lower level. As time passes the experience of a lower inflation rate will have more and more effect on expected inflation; it will therefore ultimately become compatible with a lower unemployment rate than that initially associated with it.

This theory then introduces an inter-temporal element into the inflation-unemployment trade-off. It tells us that restrictive 'demand management' policies can slow down inflation more rapidly if more unemployment is endured in the early stages of the policy and less rapidly if less unemployment is initially created. The choice is thus between slowing inflation down rapidly by having a large amount of unemployment for a relatively short time and bringing it to a halt slowly by having less unemployment but maintaining its amount for a longer period. But how much unemployment constitutes a 'large' amount? and how many years is a 'short' period?

Inflationary expectations now 'deeply embedded'
These questions can be answered only in the context of a particular economy. For Britain we may note that the (supposed)[1] existence of about a million unemployed led to a fall of about four percentage points in the inflation rate during 1972. But how far we are safe in extrapolating from this experience to the current situation in 1975 is doubtful. The current inflation rate is so high, and the recent monetary contraction has been so violent, as to put the economy far beyond the range of experience upon which our quantitative estimates of the relationships between economic variables are based. My own guess is that inflationary expectations are now so much more deeply embedded in the economy than they were in 1972 that unemployment of one million will not have so large an initial impact on the inflation rate now as it did then. And, given the speed of the current contraction, I have serious doubts about our ability to prevent unemployment going substantially above that figure in the next 18 months. Even if we prevent the current recession turning into a

[1] A critique of the official statistics is in J. B. Wood, *How Much Unemployment?*, Research Monograph 28, IEA, 1972.—ED.]

major depression, and avoid over-reacting to unemployment with expansionary ('reflationary') policies that, in bringing unemployment down, set up a yet more violent burst of inflation than we have experienced, we shall nevertheless probably see an average of a million unemployed for five years or more if we are to get the inflation rate down below, say, five per cent by 1980. If, like me, the reader regards that as too much unemployment for too long, he must reconcile himself to living with high inflation rates well into the 1980s and face the implication that the first priority of policy on inflation must be to make it possible for us to 'live with' inflation for a substantial period.

The case for indexation

This is the basis of the monetarist case for widespread indexation. It follows directly from the monetarist analysis of the 'expectations-augmented' Phillips curve. The adoption of indexation incidentally might also have the beneficial effect of enabling the process of reducing the inflation rate to work more rapidly for a given level of unemployment, although the case for its adoption in no way hinges on this effect.[1]

When the inflation rate has ultimately been brought down, will the country have to endure a permanently higher level of unemployment? If the natural rate of unemployment hypothesis is correct, it will not, for the long-run Phillips curve is then vertical. If the hypothesis is false, it will, but the permanent unemployment rate would still be lower than the rate to be endured in the interim, for the Phillips curve is certainly steeper in the long run than in the *short* run.

V

ERROR-LEARNING AND THE 'NATURAL' RATE
OF UNEMPLOYMENT

THIS QUESTION is interesting enough in its own right to make the

---

[1] In advocating indexation, monetarists are of course advocating a particular policy towards incomes. However they are not advocating an incomes policy in the usual sense of wage and price controls. It is often thought that there is something particularly appropriate about the use of wage and price controls to influence inflationary expectations. This view is fallacious. I have examined this matter in some detail, but in non-technical language, in Laidler [1971b].

natural unemployment rate hypothesis worthy of careful investigation. As Professor Friedman notes (pp. 24-25), quite a lot of research, particularly relatively early, seemed to show that the explanation was false. This is as true of Britain, where Professor Michael Parkin's *Economica* paper [1970] is particularly relevant, as it is of the United States, where Professor Robert Solow's study [1969] is, as Friedman says, widely cited.[1] Both studies used the simple error-learning hypothesis in generating a measure of the expected rate of inflation. There are two questions. First, is this procedure plausible? Second, and more important, how dependent are the results apparently achieved on this rather restrictive assumption?

On the first question, the answers now emerging in the literature seem to be that error-learning can be regarded as only a very crude approximation to the way in which expectations are formed, although useful for some purposes. It is not plausible to suppose that people will form their expectations of a variable statistic as important as the rate of inflation by using a formula that systematically leads them into error over the *long* run. Yet it is easy to show that in a wide variety of circumstances this is precisely what error-learning can do. Consider two examples: first, suppose the rate of inflation was accelerating steadily. To form expectations about it by taking a weighted average of past rates, with weights adding up to one, would lead to a systematic and increasing under-estimate. The second example is particularly relevant to British experience: would it have been sensible, after the 1967 devaluation, to form expectations of the course of the price level solely by looking back at its behaviour and taking no account of the likely future effects of devaluation on prices?

Work done recently at Manchester University has shown that, in Britain, the acceleration of inflation as well as its rate are probably taken into account in forming expectations of inflation, and that the devaluation of 1967 had an important impact on expectations. Other work suggests that the behaviour of prices abroad has had an important independent impact on wage- and price-setting in the British economy – not perhaps too surprising in so open an economy

---

[1] An earlier and little-known study by Cagan [1968] that did not rely on the error-learning hypothesis did produce evidence consistent with the natural unemployment rate explanation for both Britain and the United States.

as Britain, but a contrast with the relatively closed United States economy.[1]

Our second question concerned the implications for the interpretation of available evidence on the slope of the long-run Phillips curve, on the long-run inflation-unemployment trade-off, of making inappropriate use of the error-learning hypothesis. It is possible to show that, if error-learning is an inappropriate hypothesis about expectations, then the results of such early work as Parkin [1970] are compatible with the natural unemployment rate hypothesis and with the long-run Phillips curve being vertical (cf. Saunders and Nobay [1972]). It is also possible to show that, by modifying views of how expectations are formed along the lines set out above, the economist can produce empirical results for the British economy that positively suggest that the natural unemployment rate hypothesis is true. If it is true that the Phillips curve is vertical in the long run, and as in the United States so in Britain we are far from having a definite set of results on this issue as yet, the implications for the conduct of economic policy are serious, as I shall now argue.

VI

Post-War 'Demand Management' Intellectually False

Suppose there is indeed a natural unemployment rate. It would be that which ruled when aggregate demand and supply in the economy were in balance, so that there was neither upward nor downward pressure upon the rate of inflation. It would be determined by the way in which the geographical distribution of job vacancies was matched up with the geographical distribution of the unemployed; by the way in which the skill mix required to fill vacancies was matched by that among the unemployed: that is, by the rapidity of adjustment of supply to demand in the labour market.[2] The age distribution of the labour force would influence it, as should the educational characteristics of the labour force. Barriers or subsidies

[1] The measurement of inflationary expectations in Britain is discussed in Carlson and Parkin (forthcoming). Evidence on the influence of world prices and the exchange rate on wage and price behaviour in Britain is analysed in Laidler [1972], Parkin, Sumner and Ward [1973], and Cross and Laidler [1974].

[2] [The natural rate must also be *measured* accurately: J. B. Wood, *How Much Unemployment?*, *op. cit.*—ED.]

to geographical mobility of labour and of jobs, such as trade union restrictions, council house subsidies, etc., as well as barriers or subsidies to the acquisition of new skills, such as professional examination standards, also would affect it. It would not be a variable which could be expected to remain constant. It would be a 'natural' unemployment rate in the sense that its value was determined by the structure of the 'real' side of the economy – the institutions of the labour market, etc. – and not in the sense that it was unvarying. It would however, be *independent* of the inflation rate, and thus would not be susceptible to being altered by orthodox Keynesian, macro-economic 'demand management' policies. Only in the *short* run would an expansion of aggregate demand lead to reduced unemployment. In the *long* run the only effect would be to raise the inflation rate: in the long run the Phillips curve would be vertical.

Can the 'natural' unemployment rate be measured?
What the natural unemployment rate in the British economy might be would be extremely hard to assess: preliminary results of work in progress at Manchester University suggest that it is perhaps a little less than 2 per cent in Britain, although such an estimate is necessarily subject to a wide margin of error. But the important fundamental inference is that, if a target rate of unemployment, as set by policy-makers, lay below the natural rate it could be maintained only by repeated expansions of aggregate demand and hence at the cost of an ever-accelerating rate of inflation. The only unemployment rate that would be consistent with the maintenance of a *stable* inflation rate – and that includes a zero inflation rate – would be the natural unemployment rate. If we did not know the rate we would have no way of knowing whether the target set at any time by the authorities responsible for macro-economic policy was attainable.

The whole intellectual basis of post-war 'demand management' by government is undermined if the natural unemployment rate hypothesis is true. Policy is based on the assumption that Keynesian economics tells us how we may attain *any* level of unemployment we think desirable simply by manipulating monetary and fiscal policy. The existence of the vertical long-run Phillips curve implied by the natural unemployment rate hypothesis would force us to add a devastating qualification to this assumption, namely: *any unemploy-*

[45]

ment rate below the natural rate could be attained only at the un-bearable cost of an ultimately explosive inflation.

All post-war British Governments have given over-riding priority to the maintenance of high employment. Until the mid-1960s they seemed to be able to achieve this target with little inflation. Since the mid-1960s the record has been one of accelerating inflation. The monetarist would argue that this recent experience reflects the pursuit of an unemployment rate below the natural rate. Up to the mid-1960s he explains the apparent success of policy by Britain's link, via a fixed exchange rate, to a world economy dominated by a United States which did not begin to pursue Keynesian policies until the mid-1960s. The domestic pressure towards excessive aggregate demand coming from the pursuit of too low an unemployment target in Britain generated a secularly growing balance-of-payments deficit instead of accelerating inflation as the world economy absorbed that pressure. If this explanation is correct, the apparent successes of the 1950s and early 1960s could never have been more than temporary, for the growing balance-of-payments problem that accompanied them did not occur by coincidence but was a necessary price to be paid for running the economy at a higher level of employment than was consistent with its structure. In any event the adoption by the United States of Keynesian policies in the mid-1960s, and the breakdown of the system of fixed exchange rates that ultimately followed, mean that the conditions which made possible the high employment policies of the 1950s and early 1960s no longer exist.

Is a full employment policy possible?
Does this then mean that the pursuit of high employment must be given up as an aim of policy in this country? This is the popular caricature of the monetarist position. The implication of the natural unemployment rate hypothesis is that, if higher employment levels than are consistent with a vertical long-run Phillips curve are desired, *the way to achieve them is to operate with policies directed towards the structure of the labour market and not with 'demand management' policies.* An unemployment rate lower than the natural rate cannot be achieved, except at intolerable cost, with orthodox fiscal and monetary policy; but the natural unemployment rate can be lowered by removing barriers to labour mobility, by increasing

[46]

the educational attainments of the labour force, and so on. *Monetarist analysis suggests that it is the tools of high employment policy, rather than its goals, which must be changed.* The question that faces policy-makers is whether there is not by now enough evidence in favour of the monetarist case that it deserves to be given the benefit of the remaining doubt when it comes to finding a new intellectual basis for the conduct of macro-economic policy.

REFERENCES

CAGAN, P. [1968], 'Theories of Mild and Continuing Inflation: A Critique and Extension', in S. Rousseus (ed.), *Inflation, its Causes, Consequences and Control*, Wilton, Conn., 1968.

CARLSON, J. A., and PARKIN, J. M., 'Inflation Expectations', *Economica*, May 1975.

CROSS, R., and LAIDLER, D. E. W. [1974], 'Inflation, Excess Demand and Expectation in Fixed Exchange Rate Open Economies: Some Preliminary Empirical Results', University of Manchester – SSRC Inflation Workshop, paper 7410 (mimeo), 1974.

FRIEDMAN, M. [1968], 'The Role of Monetary Policy', *American Economic Review*, March 1968.

HICKS, J. [1974], *The Crisis in Keynesian Economics*, Oxford University Press, 1974.

KALDOR, N. [1970], 'The New Monetarism', *Lloyds Bank Review*, July 1970.

LAIDLER, D. E. W. [1971a], 'The Influence of Money on Economic Activity – A Survey of Some Current Problems', in Clayton, Gilbert and Sedgwick (eds.), *Monetary Theory and Monetary Policy in the 1970s*, Oxford University Press, London, 1971.

[1971b], 'The Phillips Curve, Expectations and Incomes Policy', in H. G. Johnson and A. R. Nobay (eds.), *The Current Inflation*, London, 1971.

[1972], 'The Current Inflation: The Problem of Explanation and the Problem of Policy', *National Westminster Bank Quarterly Review*, November 1972.

PARKIN, J. M. [1970], 'Incomes Policy: Some Further Results in the Determination of the Rate of Change of Money Wages', *Economica*, November 1970.

PARKIN, J. M., SUMNER, M., and WARD, R. [1973], 'The Effects of Excess Demand, Generalised Expectations and Wage Price Controls on Wage Inflation in the United Kingdom', University of Manchester – SSRC Inflation Workshop, paper 7402 (mimeo), 1973.

PHELPS, E. S. [1967], 'Phillips Curves, Expectations of Inflation, and Optimal Unemployment over Time', *Economica*, August 1967.

SAUNDERS, P. G., and NOBAY, A. R. [1972], 'Price Expectations, the Phillips Curve and Incomes Policy', in J. M. Parkin and M. T. Sumner (eds.), *Incomes Policy and Inflation*, Manchester University Press, 1972.

SOLOW, R. M. [1969], *Price Expectations and the Behaviour of the Price Level*, Manchester University Press, 1969.